A man is walking dow  asks God, "Why did you

God answers, "So you

Then he asks, "Why did you make women so soft?"

God answers, "So you will love them."

Then he asks, "Why did you make them so stupid?"

God answers, "So they will love you."

KAREN LORSHBOUGH

Women Who Joke Too Much

Compiled by
Silver Rose

Developed by Affinity Communications Corp.

A Perigee Book

A Perigee Book
Published by The Berkley Publishing Group
200 Madison Avenue
New York, NY 10016

Copyright © 1995 by Affinity Publishing Inc.

Book design by Richard Oriolo
Cover design by Dale Fiorillo
Cover illustration by Victor Juhasz

First edition: September 1995

Published simultaneously in Canada

Library of Congress Cataloging-in-Publication Data

Women who joke too much / [edited by] Silver Rose.
    p.   cm.
    "A Perigee Book."
    ISBN 0-399-52154-2 (pbk.)
    1. Women—Humor.   I. Rose, Silver.
PN6231.W6W65   1995   95-8210
081'.082—dc20

Printed in the United States of America

10 9 8 7 6 5 4 3 2 1

Topics

Introduction

Since the dawn of mankind women, feeling left out, have resorted to being funny to mask their overwhelming feelings of frustration ("Take my apple, please!").

For the following million-plus years, funny wasn't considered feminine. Remember the portrayal of Fanny Brice in *Funny Girl*—her quivering self-esteem and her overwhelming *relief* at having finally landed a husband? For the most part, female humor had to disguise itself as dim-wittedness. (How many people other than George Burns knew that Gracie was really the bright one?)

But just when we thought we were doomed to dumb and self-deprecating humor for eternity, along came Mae West to smash all the stereotypes. Confident, outrageously sexy and with a sharp wit that went nose-to-nose with then reigning champ W. C. Fields, she changed the face of feminine comedy forever and opened the doors for the likes of Carol Lombard, Judy Holliday, Lucille Ball and all who followed. Even Roseanne owes some portion of her swagger to this grande dame of comedy.

Today we are in the midst of a female comedy revolution (over one billion PMS jokes told!). From Phyllis Diller, the mother of all stand-ups, to Totie Fields, Moms Mabley, Elaine May, Marilyn Michaels and Joan Rivers at the advance guard, women comedians are bringing up the rear and gaining ground rapidly. When Roseanne overtook Bill Cosby with the highest-rated TV show, we had indeed arrived. Say what you will about our male-dominated society, the profit motive *always* gets the boys' attention.

We wanted to celebrate our gender's arrival with this collection of womankind's funniest quotes to date—from Mae West and Dorothy Parker to those new upstarts Rita Rudner and Paula Poundstone. If your favorites aren't represented here, please write to us so we can add them the next time.

For there *will* be a next time—the coming decades will only bring new and better one-liners, insults, quips and witticisms. *We are women, hear us joke!* The funnier half of the species will not be kept silent!

Yours in laughter,
SILVER ROSE
7299 W. 85th Street
Los Angeles, CA 90045

Aging

My mother always used to say: "The older you get, the better you get, unless you're a banana."

BETTY WHITE AS ROSE NYLUND
IN THE TV SHOW *The Golden Girls*

My grandmother's ninety. She's dating. He's ninety-three. It's going great. They never argue. They can't hear each other.

CATHY LADMAN

The real fountain of youth is to have a dirty mind.

JERRY HALL

1

My youth cream contains a secret new ingredient to keep you from aging—lies.

ZSA ZSA GABOR

At a certain age you quit lookin' behind you. I'm getting dressed, pulling up my pantyhose. I catch myself in the mirror. I look back there thinking, "My Lord! Who's that ugly man with the jowls sneakin' up on me?!"

STEPHANIE HODGE

I read an article in a magazine: women forty-nine years old having their first child. Forty-nine! I couldn't think of a better way to spend *my* golden years. What's the advantage of having a kid at forty-nine? So you can both be in diapers at the same time?

SUE KOLINSKY

I'm only seventy-five and I don't look a day younger.

PHYLLIS DILLER

I said to my old husband, "I'm gonna take you out into the country for a picnic. Do you like the country?" He said, "Sure I do. When I was a little boy, I used to live in the country." I said, "When you was a little boy *everybody* lived in the country."

MOMS MABLEY

I've been having trouble waking up. I actually dozed off at a red light. It was embarrassing, especially when the other pedestrians nudged me awake so I could cross the street.

ANITA WISE

At my age, I'm beginning to appreciate the value of naps. Sometimes now I have to take a nap to get ready for bed.

MARSHA WARFIELD

Sure, Reagan promised to take senility tests. But what if he forgets?

LORNA KERR-WALKER

The secret to staying young is to live honestly, eat slowly, and lie about your age.

LUCILLE BALL

You know you're getting old when not only can't you cut the mustard, honey, but you can't even open the jar!

LAWANDA PAGE

4

I am too old to see movies where other people die.

LILAH GARRETT

I have everything now that I had twenty years ago—except now it's all lower.

GYPSY ROSE LEE

Old age is when most of the names in your little black book are doctors.

CAROLYN COATS

5

Anatomy

In fact, I have this theory that all great men have small dicks, because there's this incredible pressure on men that they have to have this weapon, and if nature hasn't blessed them with it, they have to develop something else to make them stand out.

GINA BALLMAN

Why do men have nipples?

SILVER ROSE

Men who have everything seem to want just one thing more. They want a woman whose heart of gold beats staunchly in a thirty-eight-inch chest.

ELIZABETH KAYE

With women, the aging thing's terrible. We just fall apart. First thing that goes on you is your butt . . . *bam* . . . once it's down there it's not coming back up.

STEPHANIE HODGE

My nipples are at their prime!

SANDRA BERNHARD

Battle of the Bulge

I grew up on a big farm. Last time I was home visiting my folks I delivered a calf. I tell ya, I feel so much thinner now.

HENRIETTE MANTEL

I'm so neurotic that I worry I'll lose weight when I'm on a diet.

GRACE HODGSON

The thing I remember most about Weight Watchers was the weekly meetings . . . Every week three hundred of the fattest people in the area would gather in one room and discuss their common problem—how to get out of the room.

TOTIE FIELDS

The best way to lose weight is to get the flu and take a trip to Egypt.

ROZ LAWRENCE

Why am I bothering to eat this chocolate? I might as well just apply it directly to my thighs.

RHODA MORGENSTERN IN THE TV SHOW *Rhoda*

It's time to go on a diet when the man from Prudential offers you group insurance.

TOTIE FIELDS

I have gained and lost the same ten pounds so many times over and over again my cellulite must have déjà vu.

JANE WAGNER

It's time to go on a diet when you're standing next to your car and get a ticket for double parking.

TOTIE FIELDS

I've decided that perhaps I'm bulimic and just keep forgetting to purge.

PAULA POUNDSTONE

Give "MOM" an inch and the whole family goes on a diet.

CAROLYN COATS

You guys, you gain thirty pounds and we call you cuddly. We gain an ounce and you call us taxis. Then you don't call us at all.

CAROL SISKIND

My thighs—five more pounds and they'll be eligible for statehood.

AUDREY BUSLIK

Battle of the Sexes

During the feminist revolution, the battle lines were again simple. It was easy to tell the enemy, he was the one with the penis. This is no longer strictly true. Some men are okay now. We're allowed to like them again. We still have to keep them in line, of course, but we no longer have to shoot them on sight.

CYNTHIA HEIMEL

Why are women wearing perfumes that smell like flowers? Men don't like flowers. I've been wearing a great scent. It's called New Car Interior.

RITA RUDNER

If a woman gets nervous, she'll eat or go shopping. A man will attack a country—it's a whole other way of thinking.

ELAYNE BOOSLER

Some people don't think women can be truck drivers. Hey, I can downshift, hold my water for three hundred miles, and grow hemorrhoids just as big as the next guy!

JOAN GIBSON

You see a lot of smart guys with dumb women, but you hardly ever see a smart woman with a dumb guy.

ERICA JONG

I don't know why women want any of the things that men have when one of the things that women have is men.

COCO CHANEL

Anyone who believes that men and women have the same mind-set hasn't lived on earth.

MARGO KAUFMAN

The main difference between men and women is that men are lunatics and women are idiots.

REBECCA WEST

Beauty

I'm tired of all this nonsense about beauty being only skin-deep. That's deep enough. What do you want—an adorable pancreas?

JEAN KERR

The most common error made in matters of appearance is the belief that one should disdain the superficial and let the true beauty of one's soul shine through. If there are places on your body where this is a possibility, you are not attractive, you are leaking.

FRAN LEBOWITZ

I look just like the girl next door . . . if you happen to live next door to an amusement park.

DOLLY PARTON

Cosmetics is a boon to every woman, but a girl's best friend is still a near-sighted man.

YOKO ONO

I don't have anything against face-lifts, but I think a good rule of thumb is that it's time to stop when you look permanently frightened.

SUSAN FORFLEET

My face has been pulled up more than Jimmy Swaggart's pants.

PHYLLIS DILLER

When I go to the beauty parlor, I always use the emergency entrance. Sometimes I just go for an estimate.

PHYLLIS DILLER

Birth

I want to have children, but my friends scare me. One of my friends told me she was in labor for thirty-six hours. I don't even want to do anything that feels *good* for thirty-six hours.

RITA RUDNER

In this day and age women can have kids for other women through surrogate motherhood. Is this the ultimate favor or what? I think I'm a good friend. I'll help you move. Okay. But whatever comes out of me after nine months, I'm keeping. I don't care if it's a shoe.

SUE KOLINSKY

I think of birth as the search for a larger apartment.

RITA MAE BROWN

My obstetrician was so dumb that when I gave birth he forgot to cut the cord. For a year that kid followed me everywhere.

JOAN RIVERS

I had a Jewish delivery. They knock you out at the first pain and wake you up when the hairdresser shows.

JOAN RIVERS

My mother's version of natural childbirth was . . . she took off her makeup.

RITA RUDNER

Childbirth is painful. My sister screamed so loud she woke up the whole neighborhood . . . And that was during conception!

JOAN RIVERS

I've laid several eggs, but only two have been fertilized.

ERNESTYNE WHITE

People are giving birth underwater now. They say it's less traumatic for the baby because it's in water. Then it comes out into water. I guess it probably would be less traumatic for the baby, but certainly more traumatic for the other people in the pool.

ELAYNE BOOSLER

[Telegram to Mary Sherwood after the birth of her child] Dear Mary, we all knew you had it in you.

DOROTHY PARKER

Having a baby is like taking your lower lip and forcing it over your head.

CAROL BURNETT

Celebrities

[On Madonna] I admire her so much. She's like a breast with a boom box.

JUDY TENUTA

I didn't want to be rich. I just wanted enough to get the couch reupholstered.

KATE (MRS. ZERO) MOSTEL

I don't think Lloyd's of London would insure this mouth.

KATHIE LEE GIFFORD

Children

We all wanted babies—but did we want children?

EDA J. LESHAN

I bought a pig because I wasn't yet ready for children. I wanted something small and helpless that wouldn't require college or quality time. I figured if the pig didn't work out we could always have dinner. That's not an option with children.

JENNIFER BALL

Have children while your parents are still young enough to take care of them.

RITA RUDNER

They're all mine . . . Of course, I'd trade any one of them for a dishwasher.

ROSEANNE

My daughter is half Black and half Jewish. This means that if this were World War II, she would have to go into hiding and clean the house.

ROSEANNE KATON

I think I'd be a good mother—maybe a little overprotective. Like I would never let the kid out—of my body!

WENDY LIEBMAN

I figure that if the children are alive when I get home, I've done my job.

ROSEANNE

My husband and I are either going to buy a dog or have a child. We can't decide whether to ruin our carpet or ruin our lives.

RITA RUDNER

Cleaning your house while your kids are still growing is like shoveling the walk before it stops snowing.

PHYLLIS DILLER

Adults are always asking little kids what they want to be when they grow up 'cause they're lookin' for ideas.

PAULA POUNDSTONE

The easiest way for your children to learn about money is for you not to have any.

KATHARINE WHITEHORN

A woman came to ask the doctor if a woman should have children after thirty-five. I said thirty-five is enough for any woman!

GRACIE ALLEN

Sometimes when I look at my children I say to myself, "Lillian, you should have stayed a virgin."

LILLIAN CARTER

The real menace in dealing with a five-year-old is that in no time at all you begin to sound like a five-year-old.

JEAN KERR IN THE MOVIE *Please Don't Eat the Daisies*

There's a time when you have to explain to your children why they're born, and it's a marvelous thing if you know the reason by then.

HAZEL SCOTT

The thing about having a baby is that thereafter you have it.

JEAN KERR

It goes without saying that you should never have more children than you have car windows.

ERMA BOMBECK

Children are a comfort to us in our old age—and they help us to reach it a lot sooner.

CAROLYN COATS

I don't have any kids. Well . . . at least none that I *know* about. I'd like to have kids one day, though. I want to be called Mommy by someone other than Spanish guys in the street.

CAROL LEIFER

A Little Bit Country

There were two nice-lookin' fellers standing next to me, and one of them said to the other, ". . . That's that Minnie Pearl. . . . She carries on like she's from the country. I bet she don't know a goose from a gander." I turned around and I said, "Well, at Grinder's Switch we don't worry about that. We just put them all out there together and let 'em figure it out for themselves."

MINNIE PEARL

Of course I want you for your body. I've got a mind of my own.

JEANNIE SEELY

I woke up on the right side of the wrong bed this morning.

JEANNIE SEELY

Remember the Alamo-ny

SONG TITLE BY BARBARA FAIRCHILD

My brother bought a new mule . . . but he couldn't get the mule through the barn door because the mule's ears was too long. So brother had a saw and he was sawing off the top of the barn door to get the mule in. I said, "It's a dirt floor, why don't you just dig a trench and take the mule in that way?" And brother said, "It ain't his legs that's too long, it's his ears!"

MINNIE PEARL

He owned the biggest brussels sprout farm in East McKeesport. Well, he didn't start out to have the biggest brussels sprout farm. It's just that his cabbages never made it.

DONNA JEAN YOUNG

26

Crime

They caught the first female serial killer. But she didn't kill [the men] herself. She gained access to their apartments, hid the remote control and they killed themselves.

ELAYNE BOOSLER

I don't buy temporary insanity as a murder defense. 'Cause people kill people. That's an animal instinct. I think breaking into someone's home and ironing all their clothes is temporary insanity.

SUE KOLINSKY

At the University of Illinois they think . . . they can make fuel from horse manure. I ain't lyin'. I read it in the paper today. Now, I don't know if your car will be able to get thirty miles to the gallon, but it's sure gonna put a stop to siphoning.

BILLIE HOLIDAY

I was walking down 126th Street on my way to work. Met a fella. He said, "Moms, I *hate* this. I really *hate* this, but, Moms, gimme some money! I ain't got no home. I ain't got no family, no children, no wife! My mother, my father are dead! Moms, gimme some money! I ain't got nowhere to eat, I ain't got nowhere to sleep. I ain't got nothin', Moms. But this gun."

MOMS MABLEY

I have six locks on my door, all in a row, and when I go out I only lock every other one. 'Cause I figure no matter how long somebody stands there, picks the locks, they're always locking three.

ELAYNE BOOSLER

New Orleans is the only city in the world you go in to buy a pair of nylon stockings they want to know your head size.

BILLIE HOLIDAY

Critics

A critic is someone who never actually goes to the battle yet who afterwards comes out shooting the wounded.

TYNE DALY

I think they paid Dickens by the word.

JENNIFER BENITEZ

Confronted by an absolutely infuriating review it is sometimes helpful for the victim to do a little personal research on the critic. Is there any truth to the rumor that he had no formal education beyond the age of eleven? In any event, is he able to construct a simple English sentence? Do his participles dangle? When moved to lyricism does he write "I had a fun time"? Was he ever arrested for burglary? I don't know that you will prove anything this way, but it is perfectly harmless and quite soothing.

JEAN KERR

Asking any actor what he feels about any critic is like asking a lamppost about a dog.

JOAN COLLINS

Cynicism

No matter how cynical you get, it's impossible to keep up.

LILY TOMLIN

It takes the publishing industry so long to produce books it's no wonder so many are posthumous.

TERESSA SKELTON

Do you feel that excitement of being a woman in the nineties? Maybe it's just static cling.

RHONDA HANSOME

One of the advantages of living alone is that you don't have to wake up in the arms of a loved one.

MARION SMITH

Keep in mind that the true meaning of an individual is how he treats a person who can do him absolutely no good.

ANN LANDERS

All God's children are not beautiful. Most of God's children are, in fact, barely presentable.

FRAN LEBOWITZ

I think we all can agree racial prejudice is stupid. It really is. Because if you spend time with someone from another race and really get to know them, you can find other reasons to hate them.

BERNADETTE LUCKETT

There's nothing like a hardship song to set my toes a-tappin'.

ROSEANNE

The dying process begins the minute we are born, but it accelerates during dinner parties.

CAROL MATTHAU

If you think nobody cares whether you are alive or dead, try missing a couple of car payments.

ANN LANDERS

Dating

My Dad is an ex-cop. He used to follow me on dates with a helicopter, a spotlight and a bullhorn: "All right, out of the car, arms on the car, spread your legs . . . not you, Pam."

PAM MATTESON

Seamed stockings aren't subtle but they certainly do the job. You shouldn't wear them when out with someone you're not prepared to sleep with, since their presence is tantamount to saying, "Hi there, big fellow, please rip my clothes off at your earliest opportunity." If you really want your escort paralytic with lust, stop frequently to adjust the seams.

CYNTHIA HEIMEL

[About her deafness] I haven't had a date in two and a half years, but maybe that's because I haven't heard the phone ring.

KATHERINE BUCKLEY

I've been on so many blind dates I should get a free dog.

WENDY LIEBMAN

Whenever I want a really nice meal, I start dating again.

SUSAN HEALY

I was out on a date recently and the guy took me horseback riding. That was kind of fun, until we ran out of quarters.

SUSIE LOUCKS

I don't like dating rednecks because you can't do anything cultural with them. Take them to an art gallery, and they'll say, "This is crap." "That's a Picasso," I reply. "What about this bunch of damn squiggles?" "That's a Kandinsky." "All right, well, like in this one the guy's got a pencil neck, his nose is upside down, and his eyes are on the same side of his head." "That's a mirror."

PAM STONE

I get even with my parents. I told them I was gay. 'Cause I'm going out with this guy I know they'll hate. Now when they meet him they'll love him.

MARGARET SMITH

This guy says, "I'm perfect for you 'cause I'm a cross between a macho and a sensitive man." I said, "Oh, a gay trucker?"

JUDY TENUTA

Guys wake up at your place and expect breakfast. They don't eat bagels and M&M's in the morning. They want things like toast. I say, "I don't have those recipes."

ELAYNE BOOSLER

How many of you ever started dating someone 'cause you were too lazy to commit suicide?

JUDY TENUTA

Last week I went out with a twenty-one-year-old college student (my son is appalled, but fuck him), a graduate student, an actor, and an unemployed Irishman. None of them have a hope in hell of being Mr. Right, so I can be natural with them.

CYNTHIA HEIMEL

My social life is on the skids. I'm in such a slump. Right now I'm between *fantasies*.

CAROL SISKIND

When I think of some of the men I've slept with—if they were women, I wouldn't have had lunch with them.

CAROL SISKIND

Not calling when you're supposed to is a trait definitely attached to the Y chromosome.

CYNTHIA HEIMEL

When you're first single, you're so optimistic. At the beginning, you're like: "I want to meet a guy who's really smart, really sweet, really good-looking, has a really great career . . ." Six months later, you're like: "Lord—any mammal with a day job."

CAROL LEIFER

Death

When your life flashes before you, do you think that includes every trip you made to the bank?

CAROL LEIFER

There will be sex after death, we just won't be able to feel it.

JANE WAGNER

Funeral services were held this week for eighty-two-year-old chewing-gum magnate Philip K. Wrigley. In keeping with his last request, Wrigley's remains will be stuck to the bottom of a luncheonette counter.

JANE CURTIN IN THE TV SHOW *Saturday Night Live*

[On why she wants only female pallbearers] If those ol' boys won't take me out when I'm a-livin', I sure don't want 'em taking me out when I'm dead.

MINNIE PEARL

Death will be a great relief. No more interviews.

KATHARINE HEPBURN

[Suggested epitaph for herself] Excuse My Dust.

DOROTHY PARKER

[To coworker] God, Miles, I just wanted to have a casual conversation about death and now you go and get all morbid on me.

CANDICE BERGEN IN THE TV SHOW *Murphy Brown*

41

[On her fumbled suicide attempt] I tried using carbon monoxide, but my building has a big underground parking garage so it was taking a really long time. I had to bring along a stack of books and some snacks. People would go by and tap at the window and say, "How's that suicide coming?" And I'd say, "Pretty good, thank you, I felt drowsy earlier today."

PAULA POUNDSTONE

I'm not afraid of death. It's the make-over at the undertaker's that scares me . . . They try to make you look as lifelike as possible, which defeats the whole purpose. It's hard to feel bad for somebody who looks better than you do.

ANITA WISE

Definitions

Reality is just a crutch for people who can't cope with drugs.

LILY TOMLIN

The older I get, the simpler the definition of maturity seems: It is the length of time between when I realize someone is a jackass and when I tell them that they're one. Maybe that's why there's four years between elections.

BRETT BUTLER

Teenagers are hormones with feet.

SILVER ROSE

Infatuation is when you think that he's as sexy as Robert Redford, as smart as Henry Kissinger, as noble as Ralph Nader, as funny as Woody Allen and as athletic as Jimmy Connors. Love is when you realize that he's as sexy as Woody Allen, as smart as Jimmy Connors, as funny as Ralph Nader, as athletic as Henry Kissinger and nothing like Robert Redford, but you'll take him anyway.

JUDITH VIORST

Men are nothing but lazy lumps of drunken flesh. They crowd you in bed, get you all worked up, and then before you can say "Is that all there is?" that's all there is.

MRS. GRAVAS (LATKA'S MOTHER) IN THE TV SHOW *Taxi*

We have lived through the era when happiness was a warm puppy, and the era when happiness was a dry martini, and now we have come to the era when happiness is "knowing what your uterus looks like."

NORA EPHRON

Egotism: usually just a case of mistaken nonentity.

BARBARA STANWYCK

Rich people are just poor people with money.

BRIDGET O'DONNELL

Wit has truth in it; wise-cracking is simply calisthenics with words.

DOROTHY PARKER

Hope is that feeling you have that the feeling you have isn't permanent.

JEAN KERR

Advice is what we ask for when we already know the answer, but wish we didn't.

ERICA JONG

Condos are apartments with nice doors.

SILVER ROSE

Fear of Giants: Fee-fie-fo-bia.

VIRGINIA EBRIGHT

A father is a man who expects his children to be as good as he meant to be.

CAROLYN COATS

Anger is a lot like a piece of shredded wheat caught under your dentures. If you leave it there you'll get a blister and you gotta eat Jell-O all week. If you get rid of it, the sore heals and you feel better.

ESTELLE GETTY AS SOPHIA PETRILLO IN THE TV SHOW
The Golden Girls

The fifties were ten years of foreplay.

GERMAINE GREER

Love, the quest; marriage, the conquest; divorce, the inquest.

HELEN ROWLAND

Infinity: Time on an ego trip.

JANE WAGNER

To me the term sexual freedom meant freedom from having to have sex.

JANE WAGNER

Depression is, of course, more than the after-effects of drinking seventy-four festive eggnogs and waking up with someone whose name you didn't quite catch.

JESSICA BERENS

Divorce

What scares me about divorce is that my children might put me in a home for unwed mothers.

TERESSA SKELTON

Getting divorced just because you don't love a man is almost as silly as getting married just because you do.

ZSA ZSA GABOR

[On why she divorced James Taylor] Basically, he just wasn't willing to dress up like Louis XIV before we went to bed every night. I really demand that of a partner.

CARLY SIMON

I never hated a man enough to give him his diamonds back.

ZSA ZSA GABOR

Drinking & Drugs

I told my mother I was going to have natural childbirth. She said to me, "Linda, you've been taking drugs all your life. Why stop now?"

LINDA MALDONADO

Instant gratification takes too long.

CARRIE FISHER

Even though a number of people have tried, no one has yet found a way to drink for a living.

JEAN KERR

I never drank a drop of alcohol or took drugs and believe me, it's difficult to endure success without their help.

MARIA FELIX

You want to see drug-related violence in America? Ban all cigarettes!

SILVER ROSE

It's all right to drink like a fish—if you drink what a fish drinks.

MARY PETTIBONE POOLE

One reason I don't drink is that I want to know when I am having a good time.

NANCY ASTOR

One more drink and I'll be under the host.

DOROTHY PARKER

Bill Paley just walked into my dressing room with two bottles of champagne and opened them up and said, "Let's have a drink. Bottoms up." And I said to him, "Isn't that an awkward position?"

GRACIE ALLEN

Enemies

I don't have a warm personal enemy left. They've all died off. I miss them terribly because they helped define me.

CLARE BOOTHE LUCE

Enemies are so stimulating.

KATHARINE HEPBURN

Evolution

The trouble with the 1980s as compared with the 1970s is that teenagers no longer rebel and leave home.

MARION SMITH

At one point, Howard, we were hunters and gatherers and then it seems like all of a sudden we became partygoers.

JANE WAGNER

If evolution was worth its salt, by now it should've evolved something better than survival of the fittest. Yeah, I told 'em a better idea would be survival of the wittiest.

JANE WAGNER

Exercise

Wouldn't it be great if you really could work your ass off?

SILVER ROSE

My grandmother, she started walking five miles a day when she was sixty. She's ninety-seven today—we don't know where the hell she is.

ELLEN DEGENERES

There is a tremendous current revival of bicycling throughout the country . . . Think about it. Do you want to be known as a girl who pedals it all over town?

TOTIE FIELDS

I have to exercise in the morning before my brain figures out what I'm up to.

SILVER ROSE

The only reason I would take up jogging is so that I could hear heavy breathing again.

ERMA BOMBECK

I'm not into working out. My philosophy: No pain, no pain.

CAROL LEIFER

Fame

Perhaps one of the more noteworthy trends of our time is the occupation of buildings accompanied by the taking of hostages. The perpetrators of these deeds are generally motivated by political grievance, social injustice, and the deeply felt desire to see how they look on TV.

FRAN LEBOWITZ

I was the toast of two continents: Greenland and Australia.

DOROTHY PARKER

I'm a lousy writer; a helluva lot of people have got lousy taste.

GRACE METALIOUS

I don't care what is written about me so long as it isn't true.

DOROTHY PARKER

I never know how much of what I say is true.

BETTE MIDLER

Family

I'm an only child. My parents play backgammon for very high stakes. I used to have a brother.

RITA RUDNER

My brother is gay and my parents don't care as long as he marries a doctor.

ELAYNE BOOSLER

I wish I'd had an older sister. An older sister could have given me dating tips and told me how to put on makeup. All my brothers ever taught me was how to undo a bra with my teeth.

CAROL SISKIND

My uncle Otis was a circus strongman. He'd come out in a leopard skin and put big nails in his mouth and twist them between his teeth until they would bend. It was quite a trick, but he did look pretty ridiculous walking around with all those bent teeth!

GRACIE ALLEN

Never lend your car to anyone to whom you have given birth.

ERMA BOMBECK

I knew I was an unwanted baby when I saw that my bath toys were a toaster and a radio.

JOAN RIVERS

I never know what to get my father for his birthday. I gave him a hundred dollars and said, "Buy yourself something that will make your life easier." So he went out and bought a present for my mother.

RITA RUDNER

Once a child knows that a square millimeter is .00155 square inches, will he ever have respect for a mother who once measured the bathroom for carpeting and found out that she had enough left over to slipcover New Jersey?

ERMA BOMBECK

Children grow older not younger, and . . . while motherhood may indeed require a woman who says "yes," grandmotherhood does not.

LOIS WYSE

My grandmother was a very tough woman. She buried three husbands. Two of them were just napping.

RITA RUDNER

I was born to a nice Jewish family in Boston. I'm Lithuanian and Catholic so I have no clue how this happened!

SILVER ROSE

Excuse the mess but we live here.

ROSEANNE

Fashion

Did you see that new bathing suit they have for women now? That thong bathing suit? It has that one thin strap up the middle in the middle in the back. Puh-leeze! I spend my whole life tryin' to keep my underwear outta there, some idiot goes and designs 'em that goes there on purpose!

DIANE FORD

If high heels were so wonderful, men would be wearing them.

SUE GRAFTON

Pocket Envy is women's unfulfilled yearning for practical clothes.

CHERIS KRAMARAE & PAULA TREICHLER

Men's clothes are so much more comfortable than women's. Take their shoes—they've got room for five toes—in each shoe.

BETSY SALKIND

This wedding dress cost almost $2,000. You're supposed to wear it once? Bullshit! I wear it to work, to the toilet. . . .

CLAUDIA SHERMAN

Style is contrast: firm, man-made breasts with a soft, cashmere cardigan.

NORA DUNN

I base my fashion taste on what doesn't itch.

GILDA RADNER

Feminism

Feminism is the radical notion that women are people.

CHERIS KRAMARAE & PAULA TREICHLER

Men who teach only men should only get half pay.

DALE SPENDER

These are very confusing times. For the first time in history a woman is expected to combine: intelligence with a sharp hairdo, a raised consciousness with high heels, and an open, non-sexist relationship with a tan guy who has a great bod.

LYNDA BARRY

Remember, Ginger Rogers did everything Fred Astaire did, but she did it backwards and in high heels.

FAITH WHITTLESEY

The women's movement hasn't changed my sex life at all. It wouldn't dare.

ZSA ZSA GABOR

I'm furious about the Women's Liberationists. They keep getting up on soap-boxes and proclaiming that women are brighter than men. That's true, but it should be kept very quiet or it ruins the whole racket.

ANITA LOOS

You can't reduce women to equality because equality is a step down for most women.

CINDY ADAMS

Food

Life is too short to stuff a mushroom.

SHIRLEY CONRAN

Everything you see I owe to spaghetti.

SOPHIA LOREN

Raspberries are best not washed. After all, one must have faith in something.

ANN BATCHELDER

The first thing I remember liking that liked me back was food.

RHODA MORGENSTERN IN THE TV SHOW *Rhoda*

Chinese Food: You do not sew with a fork, and I see no reason why you should eat with knitting needles.

MISS PIGGY

I hate skinny women, especially when they say things like, "Sometimes I forget to eat." Now, I've forgotten my mother's maiden name, and my keys, but you've got to be a special kind of stupid to forget to eat!

MARSHA WARFIELD

Never eat more than you can lift.

MISS PIGGY

Isn't there any other part of the matzo you can eat?

MARILYN MONROE

Do you know on this one block you can buy croissants in five different places? There's one store called Bonjour Croissant. It makes me want to go to Paris and open a store called Hello Toast.

FRAN LEBOWITZ

Who invented cottage cheese? And how did they know when they were done? It looks like it's already been eaten. Never buy anything you have to order by the size of its curd. Of *course* it's a perfect diet food. Do you have an appetite now?

CAROL SISKIND

There are only two kinds of foods: If it's not chocolate, it's a vegetable.

CAROLE COOK

God

You know why God is a man? Because if God was a woman she would have made sperm taste like chocolate.

CARRIE SNOW

Why is it when we talk to God we're said to be praying, but when God talks to us we're schizophrenic?

LILY TOMLIN

If God gave humans four hands, would men in Las Vegas wear four pinkie rings?

LISA BIRNBACH

But it has occurred to me that God has Alzheimer's and has forgotten we exist.

LILY TOMLIN

Only God can make a paper bag.

SISTER MARY TRICKY

Hair

Where would Marilyn Monroe be if she'd clung to the hair color God gave her? We'd have a movie called "Gentlemen Prefer Mousy Brown Hair."

ADAIR LARA

I happen to have weird hair which is why I don't dress up fancy. If I dress up, people just look at me and go, "Oooh, look at her head." This way here, it's more of a total look and nobody can put their finger on quite what they think is wrong.

PAULA POUNDSTONE

I'm worried that my hair is going to get bigger than I am and take me places I don't want to go. . . .

JENNIFER HEATH

I'm not offended by all the dumb blonde jokes because I know I'm not dumb. And I also know that I'm not blonde.

DOLLY PARTON

Health

I've used up all my sick days, so I'm calling in dead.

MARY BUTCHER

I tried Flintstones vitamins. I didn't feel any better but I could stop the car with my feet.

JOAN ST. ONGE

I got a postcard from my gynecologist. It said, "Did you know it's time for your annual checkup?" No, but now my mailman does.

CATHY LADMAN

My gynecologist does jokes!
  "Dr. Schwartz at your cervix!"
  "I'm dilated to meet you!"
  "Say ahhh."
  "There's Jimmy Hoffa!"
There's no way you can get back at that son of a bitch unless you learn to throw your voice.

  JOAN RIVERS

If I am ever stuck on a respirator or a life-support system, I definitely want to be unplugged, but not 'til I get down to a size 8.

  HENRIETTE MANTEL

[On her hospital stays during her ongoing battle with multiple sclerosis] The doctors and nurses were all so good to me. As I was leaving, I asked, "Oh, how in the world will I ever be able to repay you all?" And they told me: "By check, money order, or cash."

  DONNA FARGO

Horse Sense

I stay away from the miserable people, because misery does love company. Just look at a fly strip. You never see a fly stuck there saying, "Go around. Go around!"

MARGARET SMITH

There are very few people who don't become more interesting when they stop talking.

MARY LOWRY

If you want to catch trout, don't fish in a herring barrel.

ANN LANDERS

Housework

Hi! I'm a housewife. I'm not going to vacuum 'til Sears makes one you can ride on.

ROSEANNE

My husband says I feed him like he's a god; every meal is a burnt offering.

RHONDA HANSOME

I can't cook. I use a smoke alarm as a timer.

CAROL SISKIND

Husbands

An archeologist is the best husband a woman can have; the older she gets, the more interested he is in her.

AGATHA CHRISTIE

A husband is what is left of a lover after the nerve has been extracted.

HELEN ROWLAND

My husband is German. Last night I dressed up as Poland and he invaded me.

BETTE MIDLER

The best way to get most husbands to do something is to suggest that perhaps they're too old to do it.

SHIRLEY MACLAINE

Husbands are like fires. They go out when unattended.

ZSA ZSA GABOR

My husband is living proof that women can take a joke.

SHEILA MYERS' BUMPER STICKER

I've been asked to say a couple of words about my husband, Fang. How about "short" and "cheap"?

PHYLLIS DILLER

Mrs. Tugwell just had her sixteenth young 'un. She said she had so many young 'uns she'd run out of names—to call her husband!

MINNIE PEARL

There is a vast difference between the savage and the civilized man, but it is never apparent to their wives until after breakfast.

HELEN ROWLAND

I wasn't allowed to speak while my husband was alive, and since he's been gone no one has been able to shut me up.

HEDDA HOPPER

The night of our honeymoon my husband took one look and said, "Is that all for me?"

DOLLY PARTON

There is so little difference between husbands, you might as well keep the first.

ADELA ROGERS ST. JOHN

Insults

He took my glasses off and he said, "Without your glasses, why, you're beautiful." I said, "Without my glasses, you're not half bad either."

KIT HOLLERBACH

[To heckler] Sir . . . why don't you put a condom over your head? You're acting like a dick, you might as well dress like one.

DIANE FORD

You can say I'm full of shit, but don't say I'm old.

ZSA ZSA GABOR

Nick, I'd rather be the love toy of a Greek army battalion than go out with you.

SHELLEY LONG AS DIANE CHAMBERS IN THE TV SHOW *Cheers*

Don't be humble. You're not that great.

GOLDA MEIR

Mick Jagger has child-bearing lips.

JOAN RIVERS

This is not a novel to be tossed aside lightly. It should be thrown with great force. . . .

DOROTHY PARKER

[To heckler] You bucket of lust. You make me want to have my tubes tied.

JUDY TENUTA

Irony

Some of us are becoming the men we wanted to marry.

GLORIA STEINEM

It takes a woman twenty years to make a man of her son,
and another woman twenty minutes to make a fool of him.

HELEN ROWLAND

You'd be surprised how much it costs to look this cheap.

DOLLY PARTON

It's ironic that I should be writing about bachelors,
considering I've aspired for so long to be one myself.

SANDRA BERNHARD

If you think you're too small to have an impact, try going to bed with a mosquito.

ANITA KODDICK

If you read a lot of books, you're considered well read. But if you watch a lot of TV you're not considered well viewed.

LILY TOMLIN

The less I behave like Whistler's mother, the more I look like her the morning after.

TALLULAH BANKHEAD

Why are there so many women with fake fingernails, fake eyelashes and fake boobs complaining that there are no *real* men?

GAY GOODENOUGH

We should live and learn, but by the time we've learned, it's too late to live.

CAROLYN WELLS

A man spends the first half of his life learning habits that shorten the other half.

ANN LANDERS

Life

Life is something to do when you can't get to sleep.

FRAN LEBOWITZ

If I had to live my life again I'd make all the same mistakes—only sooner.

TALLULAH BANKHEAD

I love animals and children. *People*, I could do without.

ZSA ZSA GABOR

The average, well-adjusted adult gets up at 7:30 in the morning feeling just terrible.

JEAN KERR

I often feel like I'm just circling the airport.

GRACE HODGSON

Take your life in your own hands, and what happens? A terrible thing: no one to blame.

ERICA JONG

When you get right down to it, life is the major cause of death.

BRIDGET O'DONNELL

Los Angeles

Whoever said that life begins at forty never lived in L.A.

HOLLY PALANCE

Los Angeles is seventy-two suburbs in search of a city.

DOROTHY PARKER

Hollywood is like Picasso's bathroom.

CANDICE BERGEN

Love

To fall in love you have to be in a state of mind for it to take, like a disease.

NANCY MITFORD

Love: women's eternal spring and man's eternal fall.

HELEN ROWLAND

A narcissism shared by two.

RITA MAE BROWN

If you can stay in love for more than two years, you're *on* something.

FRAN LEBOWITZ

Love is the same as like except you feel sexier. And more romantic. And also more annoyed when he talks with his mouth full. And you also resent it more when he interrupts you. And you also respect him less when he shows any weakness. And furthermore, when you ask him to pick you up at the airport and he tells you he can't do it because he's busy, it's only when you love him that you hate him.

JUDITH VIORST

Love conquers all things except poverty and toothache.

MAE WEST

Without water whales would have no place to fall in love.

SISTER MARY TRICKY

If love is the answer could you please rephrase the question?

LILY TOMLIN

Love is much nicer to be in than an automobile accident, a tight girdle, a higher tax bracket or a holding pattern over Philadelphia.

JUDITH VIORST

A man is walking down the street when he meets God.
He asks God, "Why did you make women so beautiful?"
God answers, "So you will love them."
Then he asks, "Why did you make women so soft?"
God answers, "So you will love them."
Then he asks, "Why did you make them so stupid?"
God answers, "So they will love you."

KAREN LORSHBOUGH

Makes Sense to Us!

I would love to speak a foreign language but I can't. So I grew hair under my arms instead.

SUE KOLINSKY

When I was born I was so surprised I didn't talk for a year and a half.

GRACIE ALLEN

It's not true I had nothing on. I had the radio on.

MARILYN MONROE

What's this I hear about making Puerto Rico a steak? The next thing they'll be wanting is a salad, and then a baked potato.

GILDA RADNER AS EMILY LATELLA IN THE TV SHOW
Saturday Night Live

You can lead a herring to water, but you have to walk really fast or they die.

BETTY WHITE AS ROSE NYLUND
IN THE TV SHOW *The Golden Girls*

I think I am, therefore I am, I think.

SISTER MARY TRICKY

If you close your eyes, you could just as well imagine me to be vintage Ali MacGraw, circa 1968. I'm also Candice Bergen, Julie Christie and Mary Tyler Moore in their primes. A WASP goddess bitch, cold as a ten-carat diamond just out of the vault.

SANDRA BERNHARD

Smartness runs in my family. When I went to school I was so smart my teacher was in my class for five years.

GRACIE ALLEN

Marriage

I married beneath me—all women do.

NANCY ASTOR

Marrying a man is like buying something you've been admiring for a long time in a shop window. You may love it when you get it home, but it doesn't always go with everything else in the house.

JEAN KERR

A man in love is incomplete until he is married. Then he's finished.

ZSA ZSA GABOR

My first marriage lasted eleven months. God, it seemed like a *year*!

SILVER ROSE

Men are such idiots and I married their king.

PEG BUNDY IN THE TV SHOW *Married. . . . With Children*

It's just as easy to marry a man who likes to hire help as not.

MARY GWYNN

My husband is Jewish and I'm Irish Catholic. We've decided to compromise: we raise our children Jewish, but I get to pick the names—Mary Magdalene and Sean Patrick.

JEANNIE MCBRIDE

It should be a very happy marriage—they are both so much in love with him.

IRENE THOMAS

Sex when you're married is like going to a 7-Eleven. There's not much variety, but at three in the morning, it's always there.

CAROL LEIFER

When a girl marries, she exchanges the attentions of many men for the inattention of one.

HELEN ROWLAND

The trouble with some women is that they get all excited about nothing and then marry him.

CHER

Why does a woman work ten years to change a man's habits and then complain that he's not the man she married?

BARBRA STREISAND

I've always said we got married because there was nothing on TV.

BETTE MIDLER

Men

We got new advice as to what motivated man to walk upright: to free his hands for masturbation.

JANE WAGNER

The male sex, as a sex, does not universally appeal to me. I find the men today less manly; but a woman of my age is not in a position to know exactly how manly they are.

KATHARINE HEPBURN

I like men who are prematurely wealthy.

JOAN RIVERS

A woman is a woman until the day she dies, but a man's a man only as long as he can.

MOMS MABLEY

I like men to behave like men—strong and childish.

FRANÇOISE SAGAN

I like two kinds of men: domestic and foreign.

MAE WEST

There should be a theme park based on the male ego . . . only there's not enough land.

LAURIE FROM "IT'S IN THE MALE," AN ARTICLE BY
MARGO KAUFMAN

I am the only white woman in known captivity who has not slept with Warren Beatty.

NANCY COLLINS

[Regarding the former Brooklyn Dodgers] If nine men left you and moved to another town, would you go out and root for them?

ELAYNE BOOSLER

A guy goes into a drugstore on a Friday and says, "Give me a gross of those safes." He comes back Monday and says, "There were only 143 in that gross." The clerk says, "I'm sorry I spoiled your weekend, sir."

PEARL WILLIAMS

Women speak because they wish to speak, whereas a man speaks only when driven to speech by something outside himself—like, for instance, he can't find any clean socks.

JEAN KERR

He was promiscuous by his absence.

JEAN CURTIS

If men could become pregnant, abortion would be a sacrament.

FLORYNCE KENNEDY

I could write what I know about men on the head of a pin and still have room for the yellow pages.

CHER

Money

My mother has always told me: rich or poor, it's nice to have money.

WENDY WASSERSTEIN

Money is what you'd get on beautifully without if only other people weren't so crazy about it.

MARGARET CASE HARRIMAN

The most popular labor-saving device is still money.

PHYLLIS GEORGE

Morals

I'm not bad, I'm just drawn that way.

JESSICA RABBIT (KATHLEEN TURNER)
IN THE MOVIE *Who Framed Roger Rabbit?*

I used to be a virgin, but I gave it up. There was no money in it.

MARSHA WARFIELD

That woman speaks eighteen languages and can't say no in any of them.

DOROTHY PARKER

Between two evils, I always pick the one I never tried before.

MAE WEST

[In response to, "Goodness, what beautiful diamonds!"]
Goodness had nothing to do with it, dearie!

MAE WEST

It's the good girls who keep the diaries; the bad girls never have time.

TALLULAH BANKHEAD

I'm as pure as the driven slush.

TALLULAH BANKHEAD

I guess I'm old-fashioned—I wouldn't sleep with a guy unless we were living together.

BARBARA COOPER

Mothers

My Jewish mom did not encourage creativity. On Halloween she made me go as a ghost every year, and gave me a print sheet instead of a white one. People would say: "Oh look, a percale ghost, I'm really scared."

CATHY LADMAN

[When asked why her daughter-in-law Joan lived in Boston while her son Ted lived in Virginia] Who's Virginia?

ROSE KENNEDY

When my mom got really mad, she would say, "Your butt is my meat." Not a particularly attractive phrase. And I always wondered, "Now, what wine goes with that?"

PAULA POUNDSTONE

It's not easy being a mother. If it were, fathers would do it.

BEA ARTHUR AS DOROTHY ZBORNAK
IN THE TV SHOW *The Golden Girls*

Women who miscalculate are called "mothers."

ABIGAIL VAN BUREN

You know, if you are a working mother, virtually everything that's good news for you is bad news for your kids.

NORA EPHRON

What do you get on Mother's Day if you have kids? . . . A card with flowers that are made out of pink toilet paper—a lot of pink toilet paper. You get breakfast in bed. Then you get up and fix everybody else their breakfast. And then you go to the bathroom, and you are out of toilet paper.

LIZ SCOTT

Children use up the same part of my head as poetry does.

LIBBY HOUSTON

My mother says she just wants me to be happy—doing what she wants me to do.

JULIA WILLIS

New York

I had to move to New York for health reasons. I'm extremely paranoid and New York is the only place my fears are justified.

ANITA WISE

There is no middle class in New York.

SILVER ROSE

Being a New Yorker means never having to say you're sorry.

LILY TOMLIN

Now, it is axiomatic in L.A. to say that we are isolated from one another by the tinted windshields of our Ferraris and Isuzus; in New York, we are all out in the street together fending off attack.

DEBORAH ROUNDTREE

Periods & PMS

My license plate says PMS. Nobody cuts me off.

WENDY LIEBMAN

Hello, I'm premenstrual. So I've chained myself to the radiator.

CYNTHIA HEIMEL

I went to the doctor. The doctor said, "I got some good news and I got some bad news. The good news is that you don't have premenstrual syndrome." He said, "The bad news is, you're just a bitch."

RHONDA BATES

I've been sort of crabby lately. It's that time of the month—the rent's due.

MARGARET SMITH

If you live in England and happen to have PMS when you commit a murder, you can be acquitted. England is a very enlightened country.

CYNTHIA HEIMEL

Now they're advertising breathable panty liners. You know some man invented that product. No woman would be inventing a panty liner and putting little holes in there. She'd put little tongues in there.

DIANE FORD

Pets

I'm used to dogs. When you leave them in the morning they stick their nose in the door crack and stand there like a portrait until you turn the key eight hours later. A cat would never put up with that kind of rejection. When you returned, she'd stalk you until you dozed off and then suck the air out of your body.

ERMA BOMBECK

We've got a cat called Ben Hur. We called it Ben 'til it had kittens.

SALLY POPLIN

People with spare kittens to give are as persuasive as a real estate agent with a cut-over swamp on his hands.

MARGARET COOPER GAY

Dogs come when they're called; cats take a message and get back to you.

MARY BLY

I found out why cats drink out of the toilet. My mother told me it's because it's cold in there. And I'm like: How did my mother know *that*?

WENDY LIEBMAN

I like driving around with my two dogs, especially on the freeways. I make my dogs wear little hats so I can use the carpool lanes.

MONICA PIPER

A man who was loved by 300 women singled me out to live with him. Why? I was the only one without a cat.

ELAYNE BOOSLER

Philosophy

I can't understand it. So many people fall back on faith to cope with the deeper mysteries of life. I make the waiter show me the pot before I believe it's decaf.

CANDICE BERGEN IN THE TV SHOW *Murphy Brown*

All creatures must learn to co-exist. That's why the brown bear and the field mouse can share their lives and live in harmony. Of course, they can't mate or the mice would explode.

BETTY WHITE AS ROSE NYLUND
IN THE TV SHOW *The Golden Girls*

We're only human. And being human means being an animal. And being an animal means that when another animal gets something we want, whether it be a big bone or a big boner, we have this enormous need to rip her throat out.

CYNTHIA HEIMEL

From birth to age eighteen, a girl needs good parents. From eighteen to thirty-five she needs good looks. From thirty-five to fifty-five she needs a good personality, and from fifty-five on she needs cash.

SOPHIE TUCKER

The only thing harder to get rid of than a winter cold is a 1973 Ford Pinto.

AILEEN FOSTER

I know there are people starving, and people at war . . . but I like shoes.

GRACE HODGSON

[On giving birth at age forty-one] I'll try anything once.

ALICE ROOSEVELT LONGWORTH

Politics & Politicians

[George Bush's Problem] The clothes have no emperor.

ANNA QUINDLEN

Ann Richards is smart and tough and funny and pretty, which I notice just confuses the hell out of people.

MOLLY IVINS

Ninety-eight percent of the adults in this country are decent, hard-working, honest Americans. It's the other lousy two percent that get all the publicity. But then—we elected them.

LILY TOMLIN

[On Rush Limbaugh] His new fiancee says she still loves him even after finding out how he got the name "Rush."

DIANA JORDAN

If I thought Bill Clinton could solve one problem, I would volunteer to have sex with him.

PAULA POUNDSTONE

I don't mind being regarded as perverted and unnatural, but I would die if people thought I was a Democrat.

FLORENCE KING

The reason there are so few female politicians is that it is too much trouble to put makeup on two faces.

MAUREEN MURPHY

Many people did not care for Pat Buchanan's speech; it probably sounded better in the original German.

MOLLY IVINS

Do you know what they do to soft, overweight, bald Republicans in prison, Ernest?

GOLDIE HAWN TO BRUCE WILLIS IN THE MOVIE
Death Becomes Her

Pregnancy

He tricked me into marrying him. He told me I was pregnant.

CAROL LEIFER

If I had a cock for a day I would get myself pregnant.

GERMAINE GREER

[On pregnancy] To me, life is tough enough without having someone kick you from the inside.

RITA RUDNER

If pregnancy were a book, they would cut the last two chapters.

NORA EPHRON

I'm pregnant. No need to applaud, I was asleep at the time.

JEANNIE MCBRIDE

Relationships

We're having a little disagreement. What I want is a big church wedding with bridesmaids and flowers and a no-expense-spared reception and what he wants is to break off our engagement.

SALLY POPLIN

[About Alan Jay Lerner] Marriage is Alan's way of saying good-bye.

MIA FARROW

It's like magic. When you live by yourself, all your annoying habits are gone!

MERRILL MARKOE

Whenever I dwell for any length of time on my own shortcomings, they gradually begin to seem mild, harmless, rather engaging little things, not at all like the glaring defects in other people's characters.

MARGARET HALSEY

Men say they love independence in a woman, but they don't waste a second demolishing it brick by brick.

CANDICE BERGEN

Television has proved that people will look at anything rather than each other.

ANN LANDERS

I'm not embarrassed to be with a younger man, except when I drop him off at school.

ANGIE DICKINSON

Rules

There are times not to flirt. When you're sick. When you're with children. When you're on the witness stand.

JOYCE JILLSON

Don't accept rides from strange men, and remember that all men are strange as hell.

ROBIN MORGAN

Never give up; and never, under any circumstances, no matter what, never face the facts.

RUTH GORDON

Never accept an invitation from a stranger unless he offers you candy.

LINDA FESTA

Don't allow no wierdos on the phone unless it's family.

VICKI LAWRENCE AS MAMA
IN THE TV SHOW *Mama's Family*

In the South, if you don't have an opinion, you get sent to your room.

LINDA BLOODWORTH-THOMASON

Never buy a fur from a vegetarian.

JOAN RIVERS

Never go to a doctor whose office plants have died.

ERMA BOMBECK

Sex

Women always lie to men during sex to manipulate them: "Honey, you're so big I had to order a diaphragm with an airbag."

FELICIA MICHAELS

Men always fall for frigid women because they put on the best show.

FANNY BRICE

The difference between pornography and erotica is lighting.

GLORIA LEONARD

The Walk of Shame: The walk back to your apartment in the morning in the same clothes that you wore the day before.

VANESSA VERNACCHI

I've tried several varieties of sex. The conventional position makes me claustrophobic and the others give me a stiff neck or lockjaw.

TALLULAH BANKHEAD

Sex is like supermarkets: overrated—a lot of pushing and shoving and you still come out with very little in the end.

SHIRLEY VALENTINE IN THE MOVIE OF THE SAME NAME,
ORIGINAL PLAY WRITTEN BY WILLY RUSSELL

I honestly believe there is absolutely nothing like going to bed with a good book. Or a friend who's read one.

PHYLLIS DILLER

It doesn't matter what you do in the bedroom as long as you don't do it in the street and frighten the horses.

MRS. PATRICK CAMPBELL

I used to be Snow White but I drifted.

MAE WEST

Who do atheists talk to during sex?

KAREN CHATELLE

Acting is not very hard. The most important things are to be able to laugh and cry. If I have to cry, I think of my sex life. And if I have to laugh, well, I think of my sex life.

GLENDA JACKSON

If sex is such a natural phenomenon, how come there are so many books on "how to"?

BETTE MIDLER

My reaction to porn films is as follows: After the first ten minutes, I want to go home and screw. After the first twenty minutes, I never want to screw again as long as I live.

ERICA JONG

Ducking for apples—change one letter and it's the story of my life.

DOROTHY PARKER

You call that little thing an affair?

BETTE MIDLER

P eggy, you know what a penis is; stay away from it.

BARBARA HARRIS TO KATHLEEN TURNER
IN THE MOVIE *Peggy Sue Got Married*

Sexism

I'm just a person trapped inside a woman's body.

ELAYNE BOOSLER

It's harder to get a movie made about an interesting woman than about a guy with a hangnail.

NORA EPHRON

[As a female President talking to a terrorist] "Taking hostages on a day when I'm retaining water?" This is going to go very badly for you.

ELAYNE BOOSLER

Sexual Harassment

I was reading *Cosmopolitan* and there was a woman on the cover and I thought maybe I should change my image. Maybe I should be more like the woman on the cover. How she's posed with the blouse open to the navel, the skirt slit up the side. And underneath, the caption: How to Avoid Sexual Harassment.

MAUREEN MURPHY

The robber said "Gimme your money." I said, "But I haven't got any money," so he frisked me and said, "Are you sure you ain't got any money?" I said, "Nossir, but if you'll do that again I'll write you a check."

MINNIE PEARL

Sexual harassment at work—is it a problem for the self-employed?

VICTORIA WOOD

Single

Why get married and make one man miserable when I can stay single and make thousands miserable?

CARRIE SNOW

I'm single because I was born that way.

MAE WEST

I hate singles bars. Guys come up to me and say, "Hey, cupcake, can I buy you a drink?" I say, "No, but I'll take the three bucks."

MARGARET SMITH

I took up a collection for a man in our office. But I didn't get enough money to buy one.

RUTH BUZZI

I once went for a job at one of the airlines. The interviewer asked me why I wanted to be a stewardess, and I told her it would be a great chance to meet men. I was honest about it! She looked at me and said, "But you can meet men anywhere." I said, "Strapped down?"

MARTHA RAYE

I think—therefore I'm single.

LIZZ WINSTEAD

Slogans & Sayings

Having a wonderful time. Wish I were here.

CARRIE FISHER

Once an actress, always a waitress.

COLLEEN DEWHURST

Lead me not into temptation; I can find the way myself.

RITA MAE BROWN

If at first you don't succeed, do it the way your wife told you to.

YVONNE KNEPPER

Hearst come, Hearst served.

MARION DAVIES

If you can keep your head when all about you are losing theirs, it's just possible you haven't grasped the situation.

JEAN KERR

You take romance—I'll take Jell-O.

ELLA FITZGERALD

Two is company. Three is fifty bucks.

JOAN RIVERS

I've been rich and I've been poor; rich is better.

SOPHIE TUCKER

He who laughs, lasts.

MARY PETTIBONE POOLE

To err is human—but it feels divine.

MAE WEST

Time wounds all heels.

JANE ACE

A woman without a man is like a fish without a bicycle.

GLORIA STEINEM

Vote yes on no.

ERNESTYNE WHITE

Learn from the mistakes of others; you may not live long enough to make them all yourself.

CAROLYN COATS

If You Can't Say Anything Good About Someone, Sit Right Here By Me.

ALLEGEDLY EMBROIDERED ON A CUSHION IN THE SITTING ROOM OF ALICE ROOSEVELT LONGWORTH

Sports

I have finally mastered what to do with the second tennis ball. Having small hands, I was becoming terribly self-conscious about keeping it in a can in the car while I served the first one. I noted some women tucked the second ball just inside the elastic leg of their tennis panties. I tried, but found the space already occupied by a leg. Now, I simply drop the second ball down my cleavage, giving me a chest that often stuns my opponent throughout an entire set.

ERMA BOMBECK

When it comes to sports I am not particularly interested. Generally speaking, I look upon them as dangerous and tiring activities performed by people with whom I share nothing except the right to trial by jury.

FRAN LEBOWITZ

Stuffed deer heads on walls are bad enough, but it's worse when you see them wearing dark glasses and having streamers around their necks and a hat on their antlers, because then you know they were enjoying themselves at a party when they were shot.

ELLEN DEGENERES

Talent

Being creative without talent is a bit like being a perfectionist and not being able to do anything right.

JANE WAGNER

I can hold a note as long as the Chase National Bank.

ETHEL MERMAN

Taxes

Why does a slight tax increase cost you two hundred dollars and a substantial tax cut save you thirty cents?

PEG BRACKEN

Nothing hurts more than having to pay income tax—unless it's not having an income to pay taxes on.

CAROLYN COATS

Travel

When it's three o'clock in New York, it's still 1938 in London.

BETTE MIDLER

American tourists talk so loudly so they can be heard above their clothes.

KIT HOLLERBACH

I did a picture in England one winter and it was so cold I almost got married.

SHELLEY WINTERS

Travel Arrangements: Whenever possible, avoid airlines which have anyone's first name in their titles, like Bob's International Airline or Air Fred. Companions: If you're traveling alone, beware of seatmates who by way of starting a conversation make remarks like, "I just have to talk to someone, my teeth are spying on me" or "Did you know that squirrels are the devil's oven mitts?"

MISS PIGGY

Generally speaking, the length and grandness of a hotel's name are an exact opposite reflection of its quality. Thus the Hotel Central will prove to be a clean, pleasant place in a good part of town, and the Hotel Royal Majestic-Fantastic will be a fleabag next to a topless bowling alley.

MISS PIGGY

Beware of men on airplanes. The minute a man reaches thirty thousand feet, he immediately becomes consumed by distasteful sexual fantasies which involve doing uncomfortable things in those tiny toilets. These men should not be encouraged, their fantasies are sadly low-rent and unimaginative. Affect an aloof, cool demeanor as soon as any man tries to draw you out. Unless, of course, he's the pilot.

CYNTHIA HEIMEL

Women

Seventy-two years ago women got the vote. Boy, does time fly by when you're being repressed.

LILY TOMLIN

I bank at a women's bank. It's closed three or four days a month due to cramps.

JUDY CARTER

A woman is like a tea bag. You never know how strong she is until she gets into hot water.

ELEANOR ROOSEVELT

When women go wrong, men go right after them.

MAE WEST